# Encountering Christ in The Beatitudes

## The Art of Living

### Mark Hartfiel

A Lenten Companion

*To the men of TMIY*

# CONTENTS

# INTRODUCTION

## JESUS AND THE
## BEATITUDES

The Beatitudes are not a hallmark card. They are not a quick, gimmicky, self-help, pop-psychiatry list of ways to become the best version of yourself or to find inner peace. We must resist the temptation to reduce the Beatitudes to an inward gaze alone.

"The Beatitudes depict the countenance of Jesus Christ and portray his charity" (CCC 1717). In what is known as one of the greatest proclamations in human history, Jesus is actually painting a self-portrait! With precision and clarity, he reveals and opens the inner secrets of his Sacred Heart, the blueprint to holiness and Divine Love. It is as if he is saying, "This is who I am, and this is what it takes to follow me." Jesus is asking us to become like him!

Throughout his life, every action and movement of Christ reveals his charity, but the beauty of the Beatitudes is that he unveils the precise meaning behind all his actions. He gives us a window to peer into the very nature of his inner life. We find clear manifestations throughout the Scriptures.

1.  "Blessed are the poor in spirit, for theirs is the kingdom of heaven" (Matthew 5:3).

*Jesus is poor in spirit.*

"Have this mind among yourselves, which was in Christ Jesus, who, though he was in the form of God, did not count equality with God a thing to be grasped, but emptied himself, taking the form of a servant, being born in the likeness of men" (Philippians 2:5-7).

2. "Blessed are those who mourn, for they shall be comforted" (Matthew 5:4).

*Jesus mourns for souls.*

"Jesus wept. So the Jews said, "See how he loved him!"" (John 11:35-36).

"When he saw the crowds, he had compassion for them, because they were harassed and helpless, like sheep without a shepherd" (Matthew 9:36).

3. "Blessed are the meek, for they shall inherit the earth" (Matthew 5:5).

*Jesus is meek.*

"He was oppressed, and he was afflicted, yet he opened not his mouth; like a lamb that is led to the slaughter, and like a sheep that is before its shearers ... he opened not his mouth." (Isaiah 53:7).

4. "Blessed are those who hunger and thirst for righteousness, for they shall be satisfied" (Matthew 5:6).

*Jesus hungers and thirsts for righteousness.*

"Jesus said to them, "My food is to do the will of him who sent me, and to accomplish his work" (John 4:34).

"After this Jesus, knowing that all was now finished, said, "I thirst." (John 19:28).

5. "Blessed are the merciful, for they shall obtain mercy" (Matthew 5:7).

*Jesus is merciful.*

"Jesus said, "Father, forgive them; for they know not what they do" (Luke 23:34).

6. "Blessed are the pure in heart, for they shall see God" (Matthew 5:8).

*Jesus is pure of heart.*

"I do nothing on my own authority but speak thus as the Father taught me. And he who sent me is with me; he has not left me alone, for I always do what is pleasing to him" (John 8:28-29).

7. "Blessed are the peacemakers, for they shall be called sons of God" (Matthew 5:9).

*Jesus is the Prince of Peace.*

"Jesus himself stood among them, and said to them, "Peace to you" (Luke 24:36).

8. "Blessed are those who are persecuted for righteousness' sake, for theirs is the kingdom of heaven" (Matthew 5:10).

*Jesus is persecuted falsely for the sake of the Kingdom.*

"And those who passed by derided him, wagging their heads and saying, 'You who would destroy the temple and build it in three days, save yourself! If you are the Son of God, come down from the cross.' So also the chief priests, with the scribes and elders, mocked him, saying, 'He saved others; he cannot save himself. He is the King of Israel; let him come down now from the cross, and we will believe in him'" (Matthew 27:39-42).

The Beatitudes are not just something Jesus does, but rather, who Jesus is. And this is who Jesus wants us to be as he proclaims, "Take my yoke upon you, and learn from me; for I am gentle and lowly in heart, and you will find rest for your souls" (Matthew 11:29). We must become men and women of the Beatitudes. We must embrace them and live them. If we desire to be about our Father's business, building the Kingdom of God, we can't just be hearers of the word but doers.

The eight Beatitudes are the foundation for "the art of living". As Christians, empowered and animated by the Spirit of God, our lives should reveal clear manifestations of these characteristics and virtues to the world around us. To live the Beatitudes is to become the salt of the earth and the light of the world.

Therefore, throughout this journey we must first seek to contemplate: contemplate Jesus, his countenance, his life, his actions and his words. We contemplate and then we emulate! We have to retrain our minds, and in time, our hearts and actions will follow.

In the Beatitudes, we encounter the perfect love of God and yet somehow this love ends in persecution. Jesus's love and humility is so profound that he undergoes excruciating physical torture, public mockery and he even enters into the darkness of death itself for our sake. This was his pathway, and he invites us to imitate him, giving us the sublime dignity to participate with him in the redemption of the world. He calls upon us to take up our crosses daily as followers of his way. His way is the way of the Cross. His way is the way of the Beatitudes. He gives us the Holy Spirit to follow after him.

The world will never understand the paradox of God's ways. The world will never understand the way of Divine Love. Let us do our best to enter into this Mystery and allow it to form and transform our hearts of stone.

## A Lenten Companion – Each Week Contains the Following:

1. A written reflection on a specific Beatitude.
2. A passage from Scripture.
3. Saint quotes that illuminate the Beatitude in focus.
4. A call to silent contemplation (10-15 minutes per week).
5. A call-to-action with three spiritual exercises that help live the particular Beatitude(s) in focus.
6. Three questions asked based upon your reading, contemplation, and action items.
7. An opportunity for you to journal any additional personal reflections.

### How to Best Use This Book

- This book is built with an introduction and 7 weeks of reflections and exercises. It starts with the Week of Ash Wednesday which runs from Ash Wednesday to the following Saturday. Each following week runs from Sunday to Saturday.
  - o Week of Ash Wednesday (Wednesday to Saturday) - Poor in Spirit
  - o Week 1 - Mournful and Meek (1st Week of Lent)
  - o Week 2 - Hunger and Thirst (2nd Week of Lent)
  - o Week 3 - Merciful (3rd Week of Lent)
  - o Week 4 - Pure of Heart (4th Week of Lent)
  - o Week 5 - Peacemaker (5th Week of Lent)
  - o Week 6 - Persecuted (Holy Week)
- Each week you will read and pray with the (1) written reflection, (2) Scripture passage, and (3) Saint quotes

on the Sunday that starts each week. For the week of Ash Wednesday, complete the readings on that Wednesday.

- Next, (4) take time for quiet contemplation.
- End by (5) reading the call-to-action section and consider how you can accomplish these in the coming week. If it is helpful, take some notes in the journal section on how you can accomplish the call-to-action.
- Midway through the week, re-read the call-to-actions and honestly ask yourself if you have accomplished these items. If you have, continue to incorporate them for the rest of the week. If not, make a plan to accomplish them before the end of the week.
- On Saturdays, reflect on how you did that week. (6) Read the three questions and answer them based on your experiences. If something strikes you in this process, write it down in the space provided.
- Throughout the week if anything stands out as it relates to trying to live the Beatitudes, write it down in the Thoughts and Reflections section to consider during your prayer times and end-of-week assessment.

# WEEK OF ASH WEDNESDAY: POOR IN SPIRIT

**"Blessed are the poor in spirit,
for theirs is the kingdom of heaven."
- Matthew 5:3**

## REFLECTION OF THE WEEK

Humility is more than merely a disposition of the soul but an action. Every single action of God in his creation and redemption of the world is one humble act after another. God, the Blessed Trinity, reigns on high. There is nothing on par or higher than the Blessed Trinity. Therefore, any action of God, outside of himself, is a lowering or descension. God can only move towards us in one direction - downward. The awe-inspiring act of creation is, by definition, a humble act. The revelation of his name to Moses in the burning bush is a humble act. The Incarnation is a dizzying descent from God to man and furthermore a helpless infant who becomes dependent upon his mother and father. Christ becomes a slave. He becomes sin. He takes on the curse of the Cross and bears the shame of the entire world. The author of life enters into the darkness of death. And after the Resurrection and Ascension, at Pentecost the Holy Spirit descends upon the apostles. Our prayers rise up to him like incense and our God comes down to hear them. He hides his presence in common bread and wine.

God descends to us so that we may ascend to him. This is the divine movement and the wisdom that created the world and its order. This is the paradoxical brilliance that the darkness cannot fathom or comprehend. To partake of the divine nature is to become smaller and smaller. It is to grow into a spiritual giant through a type of self-forgetfulness, selflessness, an emptying of yourself and the elevation of others.

The opposite movement continually expressed within Sacred Scripture is pride. The angel of light, Lucifer, desired to make himself like the Most High. He was intent upon ascending: "I will ascend above the heights of the clouds, I will make myself like the Most High" (Isaiah 14:14), and yet, "[he was] brought down to Sheol, to the depths of the Pit" (Isaiah 14:15). Brothers beware: "Pride goes before destruction, and a haughty spirit before a fall" (Proverbs 16:18).

The two greatest Saints in heaven, the two that have ascended to the heights of holiness and sanctity, are the two most humble in human history: Our Lady and St. Joseph. They directly counteract the pride of the Devil with the virtue of humility. They possessed heroic degrees of humility which allowed them to trample over any temptation with victory while praising God every step of the way - "My soul magnifies the Lord, and my spirit rejoices in God my Savior, for he has regarded the low estate of his handmaiden" (Luke 1:46-48).

Like water, the Holy Spirit rushes to the lowest place and fills it! Our Lady, who voices her own lowliness in the Magnificat, is filled with the Holy Spirit. She is truly "full of grace" (Luke 1:28) and overshadowed by the power of God (see Luke 1:35) because she is such a humble vessel.

Likewise, in his silence and obedience, the humility of St. Joseph manifests itself profoundly. Notice again that humility is an action. St. Joseph was a man of action. Every time we encounter Joseph in the New Testament a pattern emerges. He never speaks. He listens and hears the voice of God. He immediately responds and DOES exactly and precisely what God asks of him. With heroic humility, he sets aside any personal aspirations to fully abandon himself to the will of

God, no matter where it will lead him. Although the leader of his family, God's voice is his compass (see Matthew 1 and 2).

For Mary and Joseph, truly and profoundly this first Beatitude was fulfilled both on earth and in Heaven. For their Son IS the King of Heaven. He is the King who ushers in the kingdom. Their home at Nazareth was the Kingdom of God on earth. For wherever the King is, there is his kingdom.

## SCRIPTURE PASSAGE OF THE WEEK
*Philippians 2:1-18*

So if there is any encouragement in Christ, any incentive of love, any participation in the Spirit, any affection and sympathy, complete my joy by being of the same mind, having the same love, being in full accord and of one mind. Do nothing from selfishness or conceit, but in humility count others better than yourselves. Let each of you look not only to his own interests, but also to the interests of others. Have this mind among yourselves, which was in Christ Jesus, who, though he was in the form of God, did not count equality with God a thing to be grasped, but emptied himself, taking the form of a servant, being born in the likeness of men. And being found in human form he humbled himself and became obedient unto death, even death on a cross. Therefore, God has highly exalted him and bestowed on him the name which is above every name, that at the name of Jesus every knee should bow, in heaven and on earth and under the earth, and every tongue confess that Jesus Christ is Lord, to the glory of God the Father.

Therefore, my beloved, as you have always obeyed, so now, not only as in my presence but much more in my absence, work out your own salvation with fear and trembling; for God is at work in you, both to will and to work for his good pleasure.

Do all things without grumbling or questioning, that you may be blameless and innocent, children of God without blemish in the midst of a crooked and perverse generation, among whom you shine as lights in the world, holding fast the word of life, so that in the day of Christ I may be proud that I did not run in vain or labor in vain. Even if I am to be poured as a libation upon the sacrificial offering of your faith, I am glad and rejoice with you all. Likewise, you also should be glad and rejoice with me.

## SAINT QUOTES OF THE WEEK
### - On Humility

"Do you wish to rise? Begin by descending. You plan a tower that will pierce the clouds? Lay first the foundation of humility." - St. Augustine

"To be taken with love for a soul, God does not look on its greatness, but the greatness of its humility." - St. John of the Cross

"The way to Christ is first through humility, second through humility, and third through humility." - St. Augustine

"The soul's true greatness is in loving God and in humbling oneself in His presence, completely forgetting oneself and believing oneself to be nothing; because the Lord is great, but He is well-pleased only with the humble; He always opposes the proud." - The Blessed Virgin Mary to St. Faustina

"The most powerful weapon to conquer the devil is humility. For, as he does not know at all how to employ it, neither does he know how to defend himself from it." - St. Vincent de Paul

"It was pride that changed angels into devils; it is humility that makes men as angels." - St. Augustine

"What will be the crown of those who, humble within and humiliated without, have imitated the humility of our Savior in all its fullness!" - St. Bernadette

## CALL TO CONTEMPLATION

Spend 10-15 minutes this week in silent contemplation of the first Beatitude based upon the written reflection, passage from Scripture and powerful testimonies from the wisdom of the Saints.

## CALL TO ACTION

1. Proactively look for strengths in other people starting within your own home. Give at least one heartfelt compliment to one person every day without expecting anything in return.
2. Spend time listening to others and do it with joy.
3. Pray the Litany of Humility every day this week [pg. 61].

## QUESTIONS OF THE WEEK

How did the Holy Spirit work within you this week as you read and contemplated what it means to be "poor in spirit" and possess the virtue of humility?

_____

_____

_____

_____

_____

Which of the call-to-action items was the hardest to accomplish and why? Which had the most impact on your week and why?

_____

_____

_____

_____

_____

In what way(s) is God moving in your heart to become more humble?

_____

_____

_____

_____

_____

# WEEKLY THOUGHTS
# AND REFLECTIONS

_____

_____

_____

_____

_____

_____

_____

_____

_____

_____

_____

_____

_____

_____

_____

# 1ST WEEK OF LENT: MOURNFUL AND MEEK

"Blessed are those who mourn,
for they shall be comforted.
Blessed are the meek,
for they shall inherit the earth."
- Matthew 5:4-5

## REFLECTION OF THE WEEK

"Jesus wept" (Luke 11:35). Moved with compassion in his heart, Our Lord wept over the death of Lazarus. He mourned over the souls in Jerusalem (see Luke 19:41-44). He was sorrowful unto death in the Garden of Olives, where he perspired blood (see Luke 22:44). He mourns over our sins, illnesses and sorrows while he pleads to the Father on our behalf (see John 17).

Throughout the Gospels in multiple places, we find Jesus performing miracles "out of compassion." Compassion literally means "to suffer with" or together with another person. The Lord mourns because we, his children, mourn and thus reveals the inner heart of the Father. He longs to spiritually comfort us in our miseries and yet not make us too comfortable with the counterfeit pleasures of the earth. He understands the human heart can be tempted to settle for the things of the earth rather than the eternal embrace and comfort of Heaven.

What must it have been like for Our Lady of Sorrows to stand at the foot of the Cross and mourn the loss of her Son? What unimaginable agony that Our Lord and Our Lady endured in order to bring us the comfort of Heaven, the comfort of forgiveness, and the comfort of Divine Love.

Jesus is the Lion of Judah and the lamb led to the slaughter - the most meek and vulnerable of all. He allows himself to be falsely accused, betrayed, arrested, spit upon, scourged, tortured and mocked. In innocent meekness, he allows himself to be paraded around the city carrying the shame and curse of sin symbolized in the wood of the Cross. His own disciples couldn't stay up with him for one hour and almost all of them abandoned him. Christ, in his passion, is the icon of what it means to be meek. Yet, ironically, this is precisely how he destroys sin and death once and for all. The meekness of Christ is born out of love - a love that never fails. Death cannot hold him. *Love rises.*

Paradoxically, in our own human weakness and frailty, Our Lord is strong! St. Paul laments his own weaknesses and desperately tries to overcome them and yet comes to a deeper understanding of how his weakness actually empowers him in Christ: "Three times I besought the Lord about this, that it should leave me; but he said to me, 'My grace is sufficient for you, for my power is made perfect in weakness.' I will all the more gladly boast of my weaknesses, that the power of Christ may rest upon me" (2 Corinthians 8-9).

Let us enter into this mystery and gaze into the eyes of the Omnipotent One, the all-powerful, who at the same time is reduced to tears. He is one and the same as the man who allows the soldiers to overpower and arrest him, allows Pilate to hand him over to death, allows the weight of the Cross to overcome him and falls multiple times. He allows the crowd to jeer at him and hurl accusation after accusation without correcting them. And through it all, the all-powerful yet meek one finds it within himself to forgive them.

May we learn from his example - the awe-inspiring strength of his meekness.

# SCRIPTURE PASSAGE OF THE WEEK
### *Luke 22:39-46*

Then Jesus went with them to a place called Gethsem'ane, and he said to his disciples, "Sit here, while I go yonder and pray." And taking with him Peter and the two sons of Zeb'edee, he began to be sorrowful and troubled. Then he said to them, "My soul is very sorrowful, even to death; remain here, and watch with me." And going a little farther he fell on his face and prayed, "My Father, if it be possible, let this cup pass from me; nevertheless, not as I will, but as thou wilt." And he came to the disciples and found them sleeping; and he said to Peter, "So, could you not watch with me one hour? Watch and pray that you may not enter into temptation; the spirit indeed is willing, but the flesh is weak." Again, for the second time, he went away and prayed, "My Father, if this cannot pass unless I drink it, thy will be done." And again he came and found them sleeping, for their eyes were heavy. So, leaving them again, he went away and prayed for the third time, saying the same words. Then he came to the disciples and said to them, "Are you still sleeping and taking your rest? Behold, the hour is at hand, and the Son of man is betrayed into the hands of sinners. Rise, let us be going; see, my betrayer is at hand."

# SAINT QUOTES OF THE WEEK
## - On Suffering and Meekness

"We shall see that the tears of this century have prepared the ground for a new springtime of the human spirit." - Pope St. John Paul II

"Suffering is a great grace; through suffering the soul becomes like the Saviour; in suffering love becomes crystallized; the greater the suffering, the purer the love." - St. Faustina

"Christ endured much on the cross, and did so patiently, because when he suffered he did not threaten; he was led like a sheep to the slaughter and he did not open his mouth." - St. Thomas Aquinas

"Meekness, the greatest of virtues, is reckoned among the beatitudes. The heavenly Jerusalem, is not the spoil of warriors who have conquered, but the hoped-for inheritance of the meek, who patiently endure the evils of this life." - St. Basil the Great

"Nothing is more powerful than meekness. For as fire is extinguished by water, so a mind inflated by anger is subdued by meekness. By meekness we practice and make known our virtue, and also cause the indignation of our brother to cease." - St. John Chrysostom

"Who is the meek? Whose imitator is he? He is not the imitator of

Angels nor of Archangels, though they are most mild, and full of every virtue, but of the Lord of the universe. Paul would have us to imitate the meekness of God, that by exhibiting to us His dignity, we might be convinced that all who suffer contempt, bear contumely, or endure any other evil with mildness, controlling their anger, are imitators of God." - St. John Chrysostom

"Many appear full of mildness and sweetness as long as everything goes their own way; but the moment any contradiction or adversity arises, they are in a flame, and begin to rage like a burning mountain. Such people as these are like red-hot coals hidden under ashes. This is not the mildness which Our Lord undertook to teach us in order to make us like unto Himself." - St. Bernard of Clairvaux

## CALL TO CONTEMPLATION

Spend 10-15 minutes this week in silent contemplation of the second and third Beatitudes based upon the written reflection, passage from Scripture and powerful testimonies from the wisdom of the Saints.

## CALL TO ACTION

1.  Out of compassion for another at home or at work, accomplish a good deed in secret without ever revealing the good work you performed. Go unnoticed in this deliberate act of meekness.
2.  Do not defend yourself for every little misunderstanding or misinterpretation of your actions this week. Offer this suffering to Christ in union with the Cross he endured.
3.  Continue to pray the Litany of Humility every day this week [pg. 61].

## QUESTIONS OF THE WEEK

How did the Holy Spirit work within you this week as you read and contemplated what it means to "mourn" and be "meek" and lowly of heart?

_____

_____

_____

Which of the call-to-action items was the hardest to accomplish and why? Which had the most impact on your week and why?

_____

_____

_____

_____

_____

In what way(s) is God moving in your heart to become more meek and enter into the mourning of others?

_____

_____

_____

_____

_____

# WEEKLY THOUGHTS
# AND REFLECTIONS

_____

_____

_____

_____

_____

_____

_____

_____

_____

_____

_____

_____

_____

_____

# 2ND WEEK OF LENT: HUNGER AND THIRST

**"Blessed are those who hunger and thirst for righteousness, for they shall be satisfied."**
**- Matthew 5:6**

## REFLECTION OF THE WEEK

"Jesus, knowing that all was now finished, said (to fulfil the scripture), 'I thirst.' A bowl full of vinegar stood there; so they put a sponge full of the vinegar on hyssop and held it to his mouth. When Jesus had received the vinegar, he said, 'It is finished'; and he bowed his head and gave up his spirit" (John 19:28-30).

*Jesus lived and died with thirst.*

A thirst for union with his Father in Heaven:
"I am coming to thee. Holy Father, keep them in thy name, which thou hast given me, that they may be one, even as we are one ... I have guarded them ... But now I am coming to thee" (John 17:11-13).

"'Father, into thy hands I commit my spirit!' And having said this he breathed his last'" (Luke 23:46).

A thirst to do his Father's will:
"Jesus said to them, 'My food is to do the will of him who sent me, and to accomplish his work'" (John 4:34).

"I glorified thee on earth, having accomplished the work which thou gavest me to do" (John 17:4).

A thirst for souls:

"The glory which thou hast given me I have given to them, that they may be one even as we are one, I in them and thou in me, that they may become perfectly one, so that the world may know that thou hast sent me and hast loved them even as thou hast loved me. Father, I desire that they also, whom thou hast given me, may be with me where I am, to behold my glory which thou hast given me in thy love for me before the foundation of the world" (John 17:22-24).

Just like falling in love, the spiritual life begins with desire. In the case of Jesus Christ, we also see that it ends with desire. We too must long and thirst for something more! This desire is born from an encounter with Christ. If we have been blessed to have experienced this encounter then we are likely to be either: 1) thirsty for more, or 2) in need of rediscovering that thirst. Lord, teach me to be a saint. Set my heart on fire with desire!

This rediscovery of thirst, desire and love is precisely what the Lord pinpoints as the need for the church in Ephesus: "I know your works, your toil and your patient endurance, and how you cannot bear evil men but have tested those who call themselves apostles but are not, and found them to be false; I know you are enduring patiently and bearing up for my name's sake, and you have not grown weary. But I have this against you, that you have abandoned the love you had at first. Remember then from what you have fallen, repent and do the works you did at first" (Revelation 2:2-5).

Does your heart burn with desire for the Lord and his goodness? The good news is that wherever you are in your spiritual life, Jesus Christ wants to encounter you right there and take you further. The God who is meek and humble of heart, full of mercy and compassion, yearns to meet you right there where you stand, no matter where that is. You don't have to be a saint to set out upon this journey. But at some point, we must purge the spirit of mediocrity in the spiritual life that seems to pervade the average lay person's thoughts. The devil craves for us to live there, in this sort of complacent, lukewarm place where we are neither hot nor cold, like a race car idling on the track. Our Lord proclaims the opposite, "I came to cast fire upon the earth; and would that it were already kindled!" (Luke 12:49).

It's God's will that each one of us should become a saint and there is great reward in Heaven for those who try!

## SCRIPTURE PASSAGE OF THE WEEK
*John 17:1-26*

When Jesus had spoken these words, he lifted up his eyes to heaven and said, "Father, the hour has come; glorify thy Son that the Son may glorify thee, since thou hast given him power over all flesh, to give eternal life to all whom thou hast given him. And this is eternal life, that they know thee the only true God, and Jesus Christ whom thou hast sent. I glorified thee on earth, having accomplished the work which thou gavest me to do; and now, Father, glorify thou me in thy own presence with the glory which I had with thee before the world was made.

"I have manifested thy name to the men whom thou gavest me out of the world; thine they were, and thou gavest them to me, and they have kept thy word. Now they know that everything that thou hast given me is from thee; for I have given them the words which thou gavest me, and they have received them and know in truth that I came from thee; and they have believed that thou didst send me. I am praying for them; I am not praying for the world but for those whom thou hast given me, for they are thine; all mine are thine, and thine are mine, and I am glorified in them. And now I am no more in the world, but they are in the world, and I am coming to thee. Holy Father, keep them in thy name, which thou hast given me, that they may be one, even as we are one. While I was with them, I kept them in thy name, which thou hast given me; I have guarded them, and none of them is lost but the son of perdition, that the scripture might be fulfilled. But now I am coming to thee; and these things I speak in the world, that they may have my joy fulfilled in themselves. I have given them thy word; and the world has hated them because they are not of the world, even as I am not of the world. I do not pray that thou shouldst take them out of the world, but that thou shouldst keep them from the evil one. They are not of the world, even as I am not of the world. Sanctify them in the truth; thy word is truth. As thou didst send me into the world, so I have sent them into the world. And for their sake I consecrate myself, that they also may be consecrated in truth.

"I do not pray for these only, but also for those who believe in me through their word, that they may all be one; even as thou, Father, art in me, and I in thee, that they also may be in us, so that the world may believe that thou hast sent me. The glory which thou hast given me I have given to them, that they may be one even as we are one, I in them and thou in me, that they may become perfectly one, so that the world may know that thou hast sent me and hast loved them even as thou hast loved me. Father, I desire that they also, whom thou hast given me, may be with me where I am, to behold my glory which thou hast given me in thy love for me before the foundation of the world. O righteous Father, the world has not known thee, but I have known thee; and these know that thou hast sent me. I made known to them thy name, and I will make it known, that the love with which thou hast loved me may be in them, and I in them."

# SAINT QUOTES OF THE WEEK
## - On Hungering and Thirsting
## for Righteousness

"If I am not trying to be a saint, I am doing nothing at all ... I will not have any peace if I don't keep on trying!" - St. Dominic Savio

"Be who God meant you to be and you will set the world on fire." - St. Catherine of Siena

"Hate what the world seeks, and seek what it avoids." - St. Ignatius of Loyola

"Ponder the fact that God has made you a gardener, to root out vice and to plant virtue." - St. Catherine of Siena

"May God give us the grace to love him and to save souls for him." - St. Therese of Lisieux

"Even if we fall short in our honest and sincere attempt to reach heroic sanctity in this life, the reward will be great in Heaven." - St. Dominic Savio

"If you should at times fall, don't become discouraged and stop striving to advance. For even from this fall God will draw out good." - St. Teresa of Avila

# CALL TO CONTEMPLATION
Spend 10-15 minutes this week in silent contemplation of the fourth beatitude based upon the written reflection, passage from Scripture and powerful testimonies from the wisdom of the Saints.

# CALL TO ACTION

1. Make a deliberate act this week to separate yourself from the voices of the world and tune into the still, small voice of God by abiding in the Word of God and sacred silence. Read Scripture daily followed by silence when any passage strikes you. Allow God to burn in your heart!
2. Pray Psalm 63 (A Psalm of Ardent Desire for God) daily [pg. 62].
3. Add an extra element to your Lenten fast of food and drink this week as a recognition that your ultimate hunger and thirst is for God.

# QUESTIONS OF THE WEEK

How did the Holy Spirit work within you this week as you read and contemplated what it means to "hunger and thirst for righteousness"?

_____

_____

_____

_____

_____

Which of the call-to-action items was the hardest to accomplish and why? Which had the most impact on your week and why?

_____

_____

_____

_____

_____

In what way(s) is God moving in your heart to grow in your desire for holiness?

_____

_____

_____

_____

_____

# WEEKLY THOUGHTS
# AND REFLECTIONS

# 3RD WEEK OF LENT: MERCIFUL

**"Blessed are the merciful, for they shall obtain mercy."**
**- Matthew 5:7**

## REFLECTION OF THE WEEK

Jesus Christ is the incarnation of mercy. He is the face of mercy. He reveals the mercy of God the Father as he takes on the sins and shame of the whole world. He takes our condemnation upon himself and offers us infinite and unfathomable mercy in its place.

As Christ is dying on the Cross from asphyxiation, he has to labor intensely by lifting himself up from the nails on his feet just to gasp for a breath. Imagine the effort it would take to speak from the Cross. Yet, this was the very moment for which he came, the very reason he broke into human history to reveal the Father's love. In the final moments, he turns to the Father and utters his final prayer on our behalf, "Father, forgive them" (Luke 23:34).

These words will echo from the lips of Our Lord and into the Father's heart for all of eternity. Mercy! Mercy! Mercy! This is our greatest gift and inheritance, namely, Jesus' sacrifice on our behalf. It is a mercy that has no limits. A mercy that triumphs over every sin.

It's not until we fully understand and recognize the cost of our sin - what it cost Our Lord (his life), what it cost us (eternal separation from God), and what it sometimes costs others (broken hearts and ruined lives) - that we more fully understand the gift Christ is offering. This is what he shoulders on the way to Calvary. He shoulders the weight of the sins of the whole world and offers us his eternal glory instead. Christ takes the initiative in our journey back to the Father. He takes the infinite step to bridge the infinite gap between the holiness of Heaven and the depravity of our souls.

Our first step is simply to respond by receiving the gift of mercy with gratitude. We must allow his forgiveness into our hearts with a contrite resolution to transformation. Once we receive his mercy, we ask God for the grace to become his mercy for others. We bring light into this world of darkness by allowing the light of God's merciful love to shine through us to bring healing to a broken world. God desires to use us as his hands and feet. Jesus Christ desires to work in the world through you as he commands:

"But I say to you that hear, Love your enemies, do good to those who hate you, bless those who curse you, pray for those who abuse you. To him who strikes you on the cheek, offer the other also; and from him who takes away your cloak do not withhold your coat as well. Give to everyone who begs from you; and of him who takes away your goods do not ask them again. And as you wish that men would do to you, do so to them. If you love those who love you, what credit is that to you? For even sinners love those who love them. And if you do good to those who do good to you, what credit is that to you? For even sinners do the same. And if you lend to those from whom you hope to receive, what credit is that to you? Even sinners lend to sinners, to receive as much again. But love your enemies, and do good, and lend, expecting nothing in return; and your reward will be great, and you will be sons of the Most High; for he is kind to the ungrateful and the selfish. Be merciful, even as your Father is merciful" (Luke 6:27-36).

# SCRIPTURE PASSAGE OF THE WEEK
*Luke 15:11-32*

And he said, "There was a man who had two sons; and the younger of them said to his father, 'Father, give me the share of property that falls to me.' And he divided his living between them. Not many days later, the younger son gathered all he had and took his journey into a far country, and there he squandered his property in loose living. And when he had spent everything, a great famine arose in that country, and he began to be in want. So he went and joined himself to one of the citizens of that country, who sent him into his fields to feed swine. And he would gladly have fed on the pods that the swine ate; and no one gave him anything. But when he came to himself he said, 'How many of my father's hired servants have bread enough and to spare, but I perish here with hunger! I will arise and go to my father, and I will say to him, "Father, I have sinned against heaven and before you; I am no longer worthy to be called your son; treat me as one of your hired servants."' And he arose and came to his father. But while he was yet at a distance, his father saw him and had compassion, and ran and embraced him and kissed him. And the son said to him, 'Father, I have sinned against heaven and before you; I am no longer worthy to be called your son.' But the father said to his servants, 'Bring quickly the best robe, and put it on him; and put a ring on his hand, and shoes on his feet; and bring the fatted calf and kill it, and let us eat and make merry; for this my son was dead, and is alive again; he was lost, and is found.' And they began to make merry.

"Now his elder son was in the field; and as he came and drew near to the house, he heard music and dancing. And he called one of the servants and asked what this meant. And he said to him, 'Your brother has come, and your father has killed the fatted calf, because he has received him safe and sound.'

But he was angry and refused to go in. His father came out and entreated him, but he answered his father, 'Lo, these many years I have served you, and I never disobeyed your command; yet you never gave me a kid, that I might make merry with my friends. But when this son of yours came, who has devoured your living with harlots, you killed for him the fatted calf!' And he said to him, 'Son, you are always with me, and all that is mine is yours. It was fitting to make merry and be glad, for this your brother was dead, and is alive; he was lost, and is found.'"

## SAINT QUOTES OF THE WEEK
### - On Mercy

"Apart from the mercy of God, there is no other hope for mankind." - Pope St. John Paul II

"How happy I am to see myself imperfect and be in need of God's mercy." - St. Therese of Lisieux

"What does it cost us to say, 'My God help me! Have mercy on me!' Is there anything easier than this? And this little will suffice to save us if we be diligent in doing it." - St. Alphonsus Liguori

"All grace flows from mercy, and the last hour abounds with mercy for us. Let no one doubt concerning the goodness of God; even if a person's sins were as dark as night, God's mercy is stronger than our misery." - St. Faustina

"The Divine Heart is an ocean full of all good things, wherein poor souls can cast all their needs; it is an ocean full of joy to drown all our sadness, an ocean of humility to drown our folly, an ocean of mercy to those in distress, an ocean of love in which to submerge our poverty." - St. Margaret Mary Alacoque

"Extend your mercy towards others, so that there can be no one in need whom you meet without helping. For what hope is there for us if God should withdraw His Mercy from us?" - St. Vincent de Paul

"Two works of mercy set a person free: Forgive and you will be forgiven, and give and you will receive." - St. Augustine

## CALL TO CONTEMPLATION

Spend 10-15 minutes this week in silent contemplation of the fifth Beatitude based upon the written reflection, passage from Scripture and powerful testimonies from the wisdom of the Saints.

## CALL TO ACTION

1. Go through an official examination of conscience [pg. 63] and receive the Sacrament of Reconciliation.
2. Look up the "Corporal Works of Mercy" [pg. 65] and make a concrete plan to be merciful to others in need.
3. Ask someone for forgiveness and forgive someone who has hurt you deeply. Then pray the Our Father very slowly and deliberately while focusing on "forgive us our trespasses as we forgive those who trespass against us."

## QUESTIONS OF THE WEEK

How did the Holy Spirit work within you this week as you read and contemplated what it means to be merciful?

_____

_____

_____

_____

_____


Which of the call-to-action items was the hardest to accomplish and why? Which had the most impact on your week and why?

_____

_____

_____

_____

_____


In what way(s) is God moving in your heart to both give and receive God's mercy?

_____

_____

_____

_____

_____

# WEEKLY THOUGHTS
# AND REFLECTIONS

_____

_____

_____

_____

_____

_____

_____

_____

_____

_____

_____

_____

_____

# 4TH WEEK OF LENT: PURE OF HEART

"Blessed are the pure in heart,
for they shall see God."
- Matthew 5:8

## REFLECTION OF THE WEEK

There is no duplicity in the heart of Jesus. No division. No double motives. His head and heart, his words and deeds, his actions and emotions are all integrated together in purity. He has one motive - to accomplish the will of the Father who sent him no matter the personal cost. "When you have lifted up the Son of man, then you will know that I am he, and that I do nothing on my own authority but speak thus as the Father taught me. And he who sent me is with me; he has not left me alone, for I always do what is pleasing to him" (John 8:28-29).

The heart of Jesus was pleasing to God. This is the measure in which he calls upon our sanctification. He desires our hearts to be purified to their very core as the ancient Psalmist prays, "Let the words of my mouth and the meditation of my heart be acceptable in thy sight, O Lord, my rock and my redeemer" (Psalm 19:14).

Our Lord's promise is that the pure of heart will see God. Ever wonder why we live in an unbelieving world who no longer sees the hand of God but only sees history as one secular event after another? A world that has the vision to see amazing wonders of creation and scientific marvels yet has an ever-growing void for God? It's very simple. The world cannot see God because hearts have become corrupted, divided, filled with greed, lust, envy and pride. The world is living in blindness.

Blessed are those who can still see clearly. Blessed are those who find God in every sunrise and sunset, those who find God in the face of their children or the embrace of a loved one, those who find God in his Church and Sacraments. Happy are those who thank God for the sun and the rain and every blessing poured out upon their lives. Blessed are those whose hearts do not become divided by sex, money, power and prestige, for they will see God not only in big things, but in everything.

Besides the Sacred Heart of Jesus, the Most Chaste Heart of St. Joseph and the Immaculate Heart of Mary are the two most pure human hearts the world has ever known. Together, they are the greatest fulfillment of this Beatitude. Every day in Nazareth, they beheld the Face of God. They could literally rise in the morning and gaze upon the Face of Christ and mystically say, "Good morning, God."

Jesus Christ came so that we may know and see the Father. He came to heal and restore our hearts to purity. For all of us, this means a fair amount of purging to squeeze out the impurities, the imperfections and the disordered desires. This purging can be painful, but it has a purpose - to restore our vision and to remove the scales from our eyes. Our Lord desires to heal our blindness but his surgical pathway is our heart. Upon healing the blind man in the Gospel who had been blind since birth, the very first thing the man opens his eyes to and sees is the Face of Jesus Christ.

What do you wish to see?

## SCRIPTURE PASSAGE OF THE WEEK
*Mark 10:46-52*

And they came to Jericho; and as he was leaving Jericho with his disciples and a great multitude, Bartimae'us, a blind beggar, the son of Timae'us, was sitting by the roadside. And when he heard that it was Jesus of Nazareth, he began to cry out and say, "Jesus, Son of David, have mercy on me!" And many rebuked him, telling him to be silent; but he cried out all the more, "Son of David, have mercy on me!" And Jesus stopped and said, "Call him." And they called the blind man, saying to him, "Take heart; rise, he is calling you." And throwing off his mantle he sprang up and came to Jesus. And Jesus said to him, "What do you want me to do for you?" And the blind man said to him, "Master, let me receive my sight." And Jesus said to him, "Go your way; your faith has made you well." And immediately he received his sight and followed him on the way.

## SAINT QUOTES OF THE WEEK
### - On Purity of Heart

"Martyrdom does not consist only in dying for one's faith. Martyrdom also consists in serving God with love and purity of heart every day of one's life." - St. Jerome

"Purity is a precious jewel, and the owner of a precious stone would never dream of making a display of his riches in the presence of thieves." - St. John Bosco

"When you invoke St. Joseph, you don't have to say much. Say, 'If you were in my place, St. Joseph, what would you do?' Well, pray for this on my behalf." - St. Andre Bessette

"Only the chaste man and the chaste woman are capable of true love." - Pope St. John Paul II

"Chastity, or cleanness of heart, holds a glorious and distinguished place among the virtues, because she, alone, enables man to see God." - St. Augustine

"Work hard every day at increasing your purity of heart, which consists in appraising things and weighing them in the balance of God's will." - St. Francis de Sales

"My beloved, may every fall, even if it is a serious and habitual sin, always become for us a small step toward a higher degree of perfection. In fact, the only reason why the Immaculate permits us to fall is to cure us from our self-conceit, from our pride, to make us humble and thus make us docile to the Divine Graces." - St. Maximilian Kolbe

## CALL TO CONTEMPLATION

Spend 10-15 minutes this week in silent contemplation of the sixth Beatitude based upon the written reflection, passage from Scripture and powerful testimonies from the wisdom of the Saints.

## CALL TO ACTION

1. Give financially to a charitable organization that has enriched your life spiritually and helped purify your heart. This will help purify your heart from the temptation of riches on the one hand and help grow the organization to reach others.
2. If online images, movies, or shows are corrupting your heart and distorting your vision, get internet software to protect you and your family this week. Don't wait any longer.
3. Every day in prayer, beg God for the grace to see his invisible hand present in some small way.

## QUESTIONS OF THE WEEK

How did the Holy Spirit work within you this week as you read and contemplated what it means to be pure of heart?

_____

_____

_____

_____

Which of the call-to-action items was the hardest to accomplish and why? Which had the most impact on your week and why?

_____

_____

_____

_____

_____

In what way(s) is God moving in your heart in order to restore your spiritual vision?

_____

_____

_____

_____

# WEEKLY THOUGHTS
# AND REFLECTIONS

_____

_____

_____

_____

_____

_____

_____

_____

_____

_____

_____

_____

_____

_____

_____

# 5TH WEEK OF LENT: PEACEMAKER

**"Blessed are the peacemakers,
for they shall be called sons of God."
- Matthew 5:9**

## REFLECTION OF THE WEEK

Jesus Christ is the Prince of Peace fulfilling the prophecy of Isaiah, "The people who walked in darkness have seen a great light; those who dwelt in a land of deep darkness, on them has light shined. Thou hast multiplied the nation, thou hast increased its joy; they rejoice before thee as with joy at the harvest ...For to us a child is born, to us a son is given ... and his name will be called 'Wonderful Counselor, Mighty God, Everlasting Father, Prince of Peace'" (Isaiah 9:2-6).

The evil one comes only to steal and destroy (see John 10:10). He works relentlessly to throw at us whatever he can to attempt to steal our peace: distractions, anxieties, insecurities, vanity, worldly desires and accusations. When our focus becomes out of balance and we overly focus on the things of this world or gaze upon ourselves, it is very easy for anxiety to quickly consume our thoughts. When we turn to the Lord and cast our cares upon him, he brings us supernatural gifts and the Divine Comfort known as peace.

"Have no anxiety about anything, but in everything by prayer and supplication with thanksgiving let your requests be made known to God. And the peace of God, which passes all understanding, will keep your hearts and your minds in Christ Jesus" (Philippians 4:6-7).

Let us first experience this peace that surpasses all understanding. Imagine it surrounding you as a supernatural force field no matter what is happening in the world around you. Christ is guarding your heart! Then, let us aspire to bring this peace of Christ to others within our sphere of influence.

"Peace I leave with you; my peace I give to you; not as the world gives do I give to you. Let not your hearts be troubled, neither let them be afraid" (John 14:27). "I have said this to you, that in me you may have peace. In the world you have tribulation; but be of good cheer, I have overcome the world" (John 16:33).

Let us enter into the Prayer of St. Francis this week and pray it daily:

*Lord, make me a channel of thy peace,*
*that where there is hatred, I may bring love;*
*that where there is wrong, I may bring the spirit of forgiveness;*
*that where there is discord, I may bring harmony;*
*that where there is error, I may bring truth;*
*that where there is doubt, I may bring faith;*
*that where there is despair, I may bring hope;*
*that where there are shadows, I may bring light;*
*that where there is sadness, I may bring joy.*
*Lord, grant that I may seek rather to comfort than to be comforted;*
*to understand, than to be understood; to love, than to be loved.*
*For it is by self-forgetting that one finds. It is by forgiving that one is forgiven.*
*It is by dying that one awakens to Eternal Life. Amen.*

Take a moment to slow down and breathe deeply. Allow the peace of God to enter into your being. "Be still, and know that I am God" (Psalm 46:10). Read the following line very slowly and prayerfully:

Be still and know that I am ... Be still and know ... Be still... Be

## SCRIPTURE PASSAGE OF THE WEEK
*John 20:19-29*

On the evening of that day, the first day of the week, the doors being shut where the disciples were, for fear of the Jews, Jesus came and stood among them and said to them, "Peace be with you." When he had said this, he showed them his hands and his side. Then the disciples were glad when they saw the Lord. Jesus said to them again, "Peace be with you. As the Father has sent me, even so I send you." And when he had said this, he breathed on them, and said to them, "Receive the Holy Spirit. If you forgive the sins of any, they are forgiven; if you retain the sins of any, they are retained."

Now Thomas, one of the twelve, called the Twin, was not with them when Jesus came. So the other disciples told him, "We have seen the Lord." But he said to them, "Unless I see in his hands the print of the nails, and place my finger in the mark of the nails, and place my hand in his side, I will not believe."

Eight days later, his disciples were again in the house, and Thomas was with them. The doors were shut, but Jesus came and stood among them, and said, "Peace be with you." Then he said to Thomas, "Put your finger here, and see my hands; and put out your hand, and place it in my side; do not be faithless, but believing." Thomas answered him, "My Lord and my God!" Jesus said to him, "Have you believed because you have seen me? Blessed are those who have not seen and yet believe."

# SAINT QUOTES OF THE WEEK
### - On Peace

"Let nothing perturb you, nothing frighten you. All things pass. God does not change. Patience achieves everything." - St. Teresa of Avila

"Never be in a hurry; do everything quietly and in a calm spirit. Do not lose your inner peace for anything whatsoever, even if your whole world seems upset." - St. Francis de Sales

"If you want to make peace, you don't talk to your friends. You talk to your enemies." - St. Teresa of Calcutta

"Our souls may lose their peace and even disturb other people's, if we are always criticizing trivial actions - which are often not real defects at all, but we construed them wrongly through our ignorance of their motives." - St. Teresa of Avila

"Pray, hope, and don't worry. Worry is useless ... If certain thoughts bother you, it is the devil who causes you to worry, and not God ... Even if the world were to capsize, if everything were to become dark, hazy, tumultuous, God would still be with us." - St. Padre Pio

"Be very careful to retain peace of heart, because Satan casts his lines in troubled waters." - St. Paul of the Cross

"Acquire interior peace and a multitude will find salvation through you." - St. Seraphim of Sarov

## CALL TO CONTEMPLATION

Spend 10-15 minutes this week in silent contemplation of the seventh Beatitude based upon the written reflection, passage from Scripture and powerful testimonies from the wisdom of the Saints.

## CALL TO ACTION

1. Contemplate Jesus entering the room of the Apostles bringing peace. Like Jesus, when you enter into your home, your office or the homes of your friends this week, bring the peace of Christ to them. Smile. Be refreshing. Bring hope. Stop quarreling, stop gossiping and stop complaining. Transcend the drama of daily life, news, and politics. Be a peacemaker.

2. Take a nice long walk alone with God. Do not bring your phone unless you have to have it for an emergency. For this particular walk, don't pray the Rosary or Divine Mercy Chaplet. Instead, just have a conversation with God. Talk to him as a friend. Listen to him. Stop from time to time to recognize and take in the realities of the natural world around you such as the air you breathe, the wind, the grass, the trees, the birds, the clouds, the sun, the moon and the stars. Hear the Lord say, "Peace be with you."

3. Tell someone about the experience you had in your walk with the Lord in #2 above. Describe the supernatural peace of Christ in your own words. Gently invite them into this Divine Gift.

## QUESTIONS OF THE WEEK

How did the Holy Spirit work within you this week as you read and contemplated what it means to be a peacemaker?

_____

_____

_____

_____

Which of the call-to-action items was the hardest to accomplish and why? Which had the most impact on your week and why?

_____

_____

_____

_____

_____

In what way(s) is God moving in your heart in order to restore your peace?

_____

_____

_____

_____

# WEEKLY THOUGHTS
# AND REFLECTIONS

_____

_____

_____

_____

_____

_____

_____

_____

_____

_____

_____

_____

_____

_____

_____

# 6TH WEEK OF LENT: PERSECUTED

"Blessed are those who are persecuted for righteousness' sake,
for theirs is the kingdom of heaven.
Blessed are you when men revile you and persecute you and
utter all kinds of evil against you falsely on my account.
Rejoice and be glad, for your reward is great in heaven,
for so men persecuted the prophets who were before you."
- Matthew 5:10-12

## REFLECTION OF THE WEEK

The Cross as a Christian symbol has been sanitized. It was a Roman torture device not simply to kill a man, but to make him suffer. They perfected it as an instrument of slow death to maximize the pain. They wanted to make Our Lord suffer.

Even worse than the pain of the Cross was the shame of the Cross. It entailed the most excruciating form of humiliation they could imagine. They wanted to break his body but even worse, to crush his spirit. The Cross was a punishment for a slave and the Via Dolorosa a public spectacle of humiliation. They paraded Our Lord around the city to the most crowded streets so that everyone would see.

As if the Scourging, Carrying of the Cross, and Crucifixion weren't enough, they wanted to make sure they verbally abused him. They knelt before him and mocked his kingship, stripped him of his clothes and placed a crown of thorns on his head. He was spit upon and tormented relentlessly: "He saved others, why can't he save himself?", "Come down from the cross," "Hail King of the Jews"...

Jesus embraced the pain and suffering. Yet he did it with a hope that endured knowing the Kingdom of Heaven was at hand for him and countless souls: "Truly, I say to you, today you will be with me in Paradise" (Luke 23:43).

Jesus invited his followers to carry their cross daily. Almost all the apostles followed this very pathway of the Lord and were martyrs for the faith. They put on the mind of Christ. They followed him in persecution and experienced the glory of his resurrection. Their experience of Christ's victory over death and the reception of the Holy Spirit empowered them out of their fear and into a mission for Christ. They were willing to give up everything for the one who gave up everything for them. They understood that the worst anyone could do was take their life. But they knew and experienced the power of the Resurrection. They knew that instantaneously they would find themselves in Heaven with Christ passing from one life into the next.

"Truly, truly, I say to you, unless a grain of wheat falls into the earth and dies, it remains alone; but if it dies, it bears much fruit" (John 12:24).

"He who finds his life will lose it, and he who loses his life for my sake will find it" (Matthew 10:39).

Our families, our Church, and our world desperately await men and women of the Beatitudes. Christ is calling you by name and his words echo ever new through the ages, "Come follow me " (Matthew 19:21).

## SCRIPTURE PASSAGE OF THE WEEK
*Luke 23:13-38*

Pilate then called together the chief priests and the rulers and the people, and said to them, "You brought me this man as one who was perverting the people; and after examining him before you, behold, I did not find this man guilty of any of your charges against him; neither did Herod, for he sent him back to us. Behold, nothing deserving death has been done by him; I will therefore chastise him and release him."

But they all cried out together, "Away with this man, and release to us Barab'bas"— a man who had been thrown into prison for an insurrection started in the city, and for murder. Pilate addressed them once more, desiring to release Jesus; but they shouted out, "Crucify, crucify him!" A third time he said to them, "Why, what evil has he done? I have found in him no crime deserving death; I will therefore chastise him and release him." But they were urgent, demanding with loud cries that he should be crucified. And their voices prevailed. So Pilate gave sentence that their demand should be granted. He released the man who had been thrown into prison for insurrection and murder, whom they asked for; but Jesus he delivered up to their will.

And as they led him away, they seized one Simon of Cyre'ne, who was coming in from the country, and laid on him the cross, to carry it behind Jesus. And there followed him a great multitude of the people, and of women who bewailed and lamented him. But Jesus turning to them said, "Daughters of Jerusalem, do not weep for me, but weep for yourselves and for your children. For behold, the days are coming when they will say, 'Blessed are the barren, and the wombs that never bore, and the breasts that never gave suck!' Then they will begin to say to the mountains, 'Fall on us'; and to the hills, 'Cover us.' For if they do this when the wood is green, what will happen when it is dry?"

Two others also, who were criminals, were led away to be put to death with him. And when they came to the place which is called The Skull, there they crucified him, and the criminals, one on the right and one on the left. And Jesus said, "Father, forgive them; for they know not what they do." And they cast lots to divide his garments. And the people stood by, watching;

but the rulers scoffed at him, saying, "He saved others; let him save himself, if he is the Christ of God, his Chosen One!" The soldiers also mocked him, coming up and offering him vinegar, and saying, "If you are the King of the Jews, save yourself!" There was also an inscription over him, "This is the King of the Jews."

## SAINT QUOTES OF THE WEEK
### - On the Cross

"The cross is the school of love." - St. Maximilian Kolbe

"You must accept your cross; if you bear it courageously, it will carry you to Heaven." - St. John Vianney

"Whenever anything disagreeable or displeasing happens to you, remember Christ crucified and be silent." - St. John of the Cross

"We are co-redeemers of the world. And souls are not redeemed without the cross." - St. Teresa of the Andes

"Jesus said to me; 'How many times would you have abandoned Me, my son, if I had not crucified you. Beneath the cross, one learns love, and I do not give this to everyone, but only to those souls who are dearest to Me." - St. Padre Pio

"Apart from the cross, there is no other ladder by which we may get to heaven." - St. Rose of Lima

"The cross is the greatest gift God could bestow on His Elect on earth. There is nothing so necessary, so beneficial, so sweet, or so glorious as to suffer something for Jesus. If you suffer as you ought, the cross will become a precious yoke that Jesus will carry with you." - St. Louis de Montfort

## CALL TO CONTEMPLATION

Spend 10-15 minutes this week in silent contemplation of the eighth Beatitude based upon the written reflection, passage from Scripture and powerful testimonies from the wisdom of the Saints.

## CALL TO ACTION

1. Attend the Good Friday liturgy and offer some form of mortification to the Lord on behalf of your family, the Church, and all souls who are lost and far away from the Lord. Unite your sufferings to the Cross of Christ.

2. Offer another form of mortification and sacrifice for someone specifically the Lord places in your heart by name. Pray ardently for this person during Holy Week.

3. Celebrate the joy of Christ with your loved ones on Easter Sunday and beyond. Lent is 40 days and Easter is 50 days! Bask in the glory of the Resurrection. He is Risen! Alleluia! Let us bring the joy of the Risen One into the world!

## QUESTIONS OF THE WEEK

How did the Holy Spirit work within you this week as you read and contemplated what it means to be persecuted for his sake?

_____

_____

_____

_____

_____

Which of the call-to-action items was the hardest to accomplish and why? Which had the most impact on your week and why?

_____

_____

_____

_____

_____

In what way(s) is God moving in your heart to embrace the crosses in your life?

_____

_____

_____

_____

_____

# WEEKLY THOUGHTS
# AND REFLECTIONS

---

---

---

---

---

---

---

---

---

---

---

---

---

# APPENDIX: PRAYER RESOURCES

*Litany of Humility*:

O Jesus! meek and humble of heart ..................Hear me.
From the desire of being esteemed .......... Deliver me, Jesus.
From the desire of being loved ...............Deliver me, Jesus.
From the desire of being extolled ............Deliver me, Jesus.
From the desire of being honored .......... Deliver me, Jesus.
From the desire of being praised ............. Deliver me, Jesus.
From the desire of being preferred to others. Deliver me, Jesus.
From the desire of being consulted .......... Deliver me, Jesus.
From the desire of being approved .......... Deliver me, Jesus.
From the fear of being humiliated .......... Deliver me, Jesus.
From the fear of being despised .............. Deliver me, Jesus.
From the fear of suffering rebukes .......... Deliver me, Jesus.
From the fear of being calumniated ..........Deliver me, Jesus.
From the fear of being forgotten ......... Deliver me, Jesus
From the fear of being ridiculed ............. Deliver me, Jesus.
From the fear of being wronged ............. Deliver me, Jesus.
From the fear of being suspected ............ Deliver me, Jesus.

That others may be loved more than I, Jesus, grant me the grace to desire it.

That others may be esteemed more than I, Jesus, grant me the grace to desire it.

That, in the opinion of the world, others may increase and I may decrease, Jesus, grant me the grace to desire it.

That others may be chosen and I set aside, Jesus, grant me the grace to desire it.

That others may be praised and I unnoticed, Jesus, grant me the grace to desire it.

That others may be preferred to me in everything, Jesus, grant me the grace to desire it.

That others may become holier than I, provided that I may become as holy as I should, Jesus, grant me the grace to desire it.

Amen

*Psalm 63:*

O God, thou art my God, I seek thee, my soul thirsts for thee; my flesh faints for thee, as in a dry and weary land where no water is. So I have looked upon thee in the sanctuary, beholding thy power and glory. Because thy steadfast love is better than life, my lips will praise thee. So I will bless thee as long as I live; I will lift up my hands and call on thy name.

My soul is feasted as with marrow and fat, and my mouth praises thee with joyful lips, when I think of thee upon my bed, and meditate on thee in the watches of the night; for thou hast been my help, and in the shadow of thy wings I sing for joy. My soul clings to thee; thy right hand upholds me.

But those who seek to destroy my life shall go down into the depths of the earth; they shall be given over to the power of the sword, they shall be prey for jackals. But the king shall rejoice in God; all who swear by him shall glory; for the mouths of liars will be stopped.

*Examination of Conscious*: (Source EWTN, USCCB and CCC)

## I. "I am the Lord, thy God, thou shalt not have strange gods before Me."

Have I treated people, events, or things as more important than God?

## II. "Thou shalt not take the name of the Lord thy God in vain."

Have my words, actively or passively, put down God, the Church, or people?

## III. Remember to keep holy the Sabbath day.

Do I go to Mass every Sunday (or Saturday Vigil) and on Holy Days of Obligation? Do I avoid, when possible, work that impedes worship to God, joy for the Lord's Day, and proper relaxation of mind and body? Do I look for ways to spend time with family or in service on Sunday?

## IV. Honor thy Father and Mother.

Parents: Have I set a bad example for my children by casually missing Mass, neglecting prayer, or ignoring my responsibility to provide a Catholic education by either sending my children to parochial school or to C.C.D. (Religious Education Program)? Do I show little or no interest in my children's faith and practice of it?

Children: Do I show my parents due respect? Do I seek to maintain good communication with my parents where possible? Do I criticize them for lacking skills I think they should have?

## V. Thou shalt not kill.

Have I harmed another through physical, verbal, or emotional means, including gossip or manipulation of any kind?

## VI. Thou shalt not commit adultery.

Have I committed adultery? Adultery primarily refers to marital infidelity. When two partners, of whom at least one is married to another party, have sexual relations - they commit adultery. He who commits adultery fails in his commitment. He does injury to the sign of the covenant which the marriage bond is, transgresses the rights of the other spouse, and undermines the institution of marriage by breaking the contract on which it is based. He compromises the good of human generation and the welfare of children who need their parents' stable union.

Have I respected the physical and sexual dignity of others and of myself?

## VII. Thou shalt not steal.

Have I taken or wasted time or resources that belonged to another? The seventh commandment forbids unjustly taking or keeping the goods of one's neighbor and wronging him in any way with respect to his goods.

## VIII. Thou shalt not bear false witness against thy neighbor.

Have I gossiped, told lies, or embellished stories at the expense of another?

## IX. Thou shalt not covet thy neighbor's wife.

Have I honored my spouse with my full affection and exclusive love? Do I view pornographic material? Have I gone to massage parlors, strip clubs, or adult bookstores? Did I commit the sins of masturbation and/or artificial contraception? Have I not avoided the occasions of sin (persons or places) which would tempt me to be unfaithful to my spouse or to my own chastity? Do I encourage and entertain impure thoughts and desires? Do I tell or listen to dirty jokes? Have I committed fornication?

## X. Thou shalt not covet thy neighbor's goods.

Have I stolen any object, committed any shoplifting or cheated anyone of their money? Did I knowingly deceive someone in business or commit fraud? Have I shown disrespect or even contempt for other people's property? Have I done any acts of vandalism? Am I greedy or envious of another's goods? Do I let financial and material concerns or the desire for comfort override my duty to God, to Church, to my family or my own spiritual well-being?

## Corporal Works of Mercy: CCC 2447

*"The works of mercy* are charitable actions by which we come to the aid of our neighbor in his spiritual and bodily necessities. Instructing, advising, consoling, comforting are spiritual works of mercy, as are forgiving and bearing wrongs patiently. The corporal works of mercy consist especially in feeding the hungry, sheltering the homeless, clothing the naked, visiting the sick and imprisoned, and burying the dead. Among all these, giving alms to the poor is one of the chief witnesses to fraternal charity: it is also a work of justice pleasing to God.

# ABOUT THE AUTHOR

Mark Hartfiel is the Vice-President of Paradisus Dei. For over 15 years, Mark has worked tirelessly to help thousands of men recognize their calling as authentic leaders in their marriages and families through the *That Man is You!* men's program. He is the current developer and host of *That Man Is You!*

Mark is the author of three additional books:

- *The School of Nazareth: A Spiritual Journey with St. Joseph*
- *Into Great Freedom: From Purgation to Illumination*
- *The Hinge of the Hail Mary: The Art of Praying the Rosary*

Mark and his family live in Houston, Texas.